PICK ME LAST
A play by Idris Goodwin

LICENSING & PRODUCTION INQUIRIES
Uproar Theatrics, LLC.
hello@uproartheatrics.com | www.UproarTheatrics.com

Pick Me Last was originally commissioned and produced by La Jolla Playhouse
Christopher Ashley, Artistic Director & Debby Buchholz, Managing Director

Chavonne, 11 going on 12
Wes, solidly 12

A CHORUS (as few as 3 or as many as you need) TO
EMBODY

Team Captain Claire
Team Captain Bilal
New Kid

Esme
Zora
Corey
Stacy Stenographer
Richie

Freud
Edward Lorenz
Grace Hopper

Mr. Burger
Mr. Yancy
TWFTPOTPWRA (Teacher Who For The Purposes Of This
Play Will Remain Anonymous)

Stranger 1
Stranger 2

+anybody I may have forgotten

A NOTE FROM THE PLAYWRIGHT:

Italics denote a shift to verse, to rhythmic speech.

CHAVONNE

If you eat cornbread in your bed it can cause a fender bender.
Don't believe me? I learned the hard way.

When I was real little, I couldn't get to sleep until I had *a
just-before-bed-snack*
Corn bread worked every time. My mother makes the best
cornbread.

But when I got a little older she told me, "You're a big girl
now and can get to sleep without eating a snack."

So--here's what I did. Sunday dinners, I'd sneak the corn
bread in my napkin for later

And just before lights out I'd gobble it up.

But, as you can imagine, you're gonna get a lot of crumbs.
And because I'm not supposed to be eating cornbread in bed,
I would push the crumbs off the sheets and under my bed

And guess who showed up?

Ants, lots of ants

And after they get through with crumbs under the bed guess
where they go looking for more? Over the bed and guess
who's in the bed?

Me!
Ants!
I felt tons of little tiny legs and pinchers all over me.

AHHHH!

And then my mother and father rushed in

MOTHER & FATHER

AHHHH
What?
What?
Ants!
Ants?!
ANTS!

AHHHHH!!!

CHAVONNE

Who can go back to sleep after that?
Now everyone is up because of me

Did you know one of the leading causes of fender benders is
fatigue?
And Mom and Dad wake up cranky and groggy

My dad was running late, spilled coffee on his uniform
And forgot his lunch

And sure enough *bang*!
Rear ended another car and got whiplash and had to wear a
neck brace for months

Why?

Because I ate cornbread in bed
Which brought the ants
Which caused me to scream in the middle of the night
Causing them to wake up
Causing them to scream

CHAVONNE (cont)

Causing them to become ad hoc exterminators
And not be able to get back to sleep
Causing the fatigue that led to him not noticing the car in
front of him had hit their brakes and *wham-o*

That's what they call a butterfly effect

MRS. YANCY

Although the concept of the butterfly effect has long been
debated, the identification of it as a distinct effect is credited
to American mathematician and meteorologist Edward
Lorenz

EDWARD LORENZ

The E
The D
The W-A
The R
THE D

Lorenz last name

It's Edddddiiiiiieeee

What's up?

MRS. YANCY

Wait wait...There is no evidence that Mr. Lorenz behaved in
this way

EDWARD LORENZ

Behaved like what?

MRS. YANCY

You know…

EDWARD LORENZ

Show's what you know
I was all about flow
The scientific terrific mathematically proficient pro-fess-or

MRS.YANCY

Well I was going to share something you wrote in your
seminal publication on the subject

EDWARD LORENZ

Oh you mean….(spoken quickly in three sustained breaths)

> Subject to the conditions of uniqueness, continuity,
> and boundedness, which in a certain sense is free of
> transient properties, is unstable if it is nonperiodic. If
> it is stable at all, its very stability is one of its
> transient properties, which tends to die out as time
> progresses. All non-periodic trajectories are
> effectively unstable from the point of view of
> practical prediction.

Nah they don't wanna hear that---here's a better way of
saying it:

Even the smallest change can make the biggest impact

CHAVONNE

Like if you move the decimal one place

MRS. YANCY

At 33 degrees the water is still liquid but at 32 degrees its
frozen

LORENZ

Exact-a-mundo! If a butterfly flaps their wings it could
make an earthquake in Japan!

CHAVONNE

Or a girl eats cornbread in her bed and dad has a car
accident!

CHAVONNE

Why am I telling you this? Because--today they're gonna be
picking teams
Everyday at recess we play either kick ball or dodgeball or
basketball or softball
Our Team Captains--Bilal and Claire never change. They
will always decide.

TEAM CAPTAIN BILAL

I'll take Isis

TEAM CAPTAIN CLAIRE

I'll take Tim

CHAVONNE

The game doesn't matter

TEAM CAPTAIN BILAL

I'll take Hector

TEAM CAPTAIN CLAIRE

Julia

CHAVONNE
The same kids are always picked in almost always the same
order

TEAM CAPTAIN BILAL
Quincy

CHAVONNE
Every day it follows the same script
every time, the final two

TEAM CAPTAIN CLAIRE
Uhhh Chavonne

TEAM CAPTAIN BILAL
Yeah okay--I guess I'll take Wes

CHAVONNE
Me, I could care less, I'm either third or second to last
It's no mystery, I'm into science and social studies
I'm just here for the fun and the cardio
 but Wes here--he gets picked last every time

WES
Softball
Kickball
Basketball
Dodgeball

CHAVONNE
All the balls
All the games
Always last
For as long as Wes has been eligible to be picked
And I have known Wes a long time
He is consistently picked last

TEAM CAPTAIN BILAL
Look, when you're a team captain you have a responsibility
You have to assemble a team that'll get results

TEAM CAPTAIN CLAIRE
Speed
Agility
Endurance
Strength
Reflexes

TEAM CAPTAIN BILAL
We're not here to make friends

TEAM CAPTAIN CLAIRE
Making friends would be kinda nice but yes it's about
winning

◇◇◇◇◇◇◇

CHAVONNE
Speaking of which

NEW KID
Hi

CHAVONNE
Uh Hi

NEW KID
I'm new to your school. Yup just moved here.

CHAVONNE
Oh, well, welcome

NEW KIDS

Thanks. Quite some—

CHAVONNE

Sorry to cut you off---kind of in the middle of something

NEW KID

Oh Okay. See ya.

CHAVONNE

Anyway--You may not think its that big a deal but just like
the wings of that butterfly
Every action has a reaction
 I read this article one time from this famous important
woman, an ambassador or something. She said she's never
forgotten how she was always the last to be chosen for a
team. She said it made her embarrassed and feel pathetic.

And it would be a shame for Wes to feel that way

Wes is not fast
Or agile
Or ---endured--i don't know what endurance means--who
says that
His reflexes are---you see where I'm going with this
But he is strong--not like The Hulk strong but he's got his
own type of powers
I remember the day I realized it---

Y'all ready for a flashback?

FREUD

What it do! It's ya man Sigmund Freud! Father of modern psychology and whatnot

MRS. YANCY

Uuuuuuhhhmmmm….I am fairly certain Sigmund Freud the father of modern psychology didn't refer to himself as…."ya man"

CHAVONNE

Shhhh--I want to use this opportunity to educate folks on the neuro science of the flashback

MRS. YANCY

Well obviously, I have no problem with educating people BUT we must be accurate when…

FREUD

Flaaaaaashback

CHAVONNE

Flaaaaaaaaashback

WES

I love a good flashback

FREUD

So yo--peep!

Flashbacks may seem random at first. They can be triggered by fairly ordinary experiences connected with the senses, like the smell of someone's odor or a particular tone of voice.

CHAVONNE

Flashback! 2nd grade! Mr. Burger's class

MR. BURGER

Good morning class!

CLASS

Good morning Mr. Burger

MR. BURGER

Our theme for the week is becoming a solutionary
And Your assignment was to find a common problem in your house
And come up with a solution.
Who wants to go fi--

ESME

Me Mr. Burger, I'm ready

MR. BURGER

Uhmm--remember Esme we are gonna let someone else try and go first for a change

ESME

But I'm ready now

MR. BURGER

Well first would anyone else like to go first?

We wait for a millisecond

ESME

See. no one!

ESME

Okay, so at my house. We have three dogs. They're all pugs. And as you can imagine, they need a lot of walking and feeding. And that's my job. Because I'm the one who asked for them all, all three. It had to be three.

So the deal was that if I got all three I had to be in charge of walking them and feeding them and I was at first. For a while but then....I forgot a few times. Not a lot. A few times. So my solution is what if there was a robot who would walk the dogs and feed the dogs?

CHAVONNE

Oh and I should just say--I know it's not about me right now. But just for the record
Mr. Burger specifically told the group, NO saying that a robot is your solution. The solutions have to be non robot oriented. But to be fair, Esme was not the only one

MR.BURGER

Richie

RICHIE

My solution to the global warming is what if we just got robots to

MR. BURGER

Zora

ZORA

My solution to homelessness is what if we got robots to

MR. BURGER

Corey

COREY

my solution? Robots!

CHORUS

 my solution, robots
my solution, robots
my solution, robots.

CHAVONNE

There was only one who was robot free

MR. BURGER

Wes

WES

The biggest problem in the house is that its very very loud
Television, Phones, My parents
They yell at the television
At the phone

.

.

.

At each other. At me sometimes--So I keep quiet--best I can

But really my solution ---I like to play music. Afro Beat,
that's my favorite kind. People like Fela Kuti and Antibalas--
it's fun. And my parents would say, *turn that down!* or *turn
that off I'm on the phone!*

I'd wear headphones and then they'd call for me *Wes, come
down here and pick up your jacket*
Wes time to eat
Wes come talk to your grandfather
And I wouldn't hear them so they said no more headphones
in the house.....

So my solution I learned to hear the music, start to finish,
every song, all the afrobeat I want---without headphones and
without turning on the spotify.

                    WES (cont)
I just close my eyes and I…

             Wes begins to sway as he listens and hums

Over the CNN and MSNBC and NPR
Over mom and dad's clients on the video conference
And then they call for me--I hear them--my name is what'll
snap me out of it

My solution--I can hear the music on my own.

                   MR. BURGER
Uhmm---lets give Wes a round of applause

                   CHAVONNE
People heard that---and they thought it was a little weird. I
didn't--we all hear music
But they started calling him Jukebox Johnny

◇◇◇◇◇◇◇

                   CHAVONNE
Hi

                     WES
Hi

                   CHAVONNE
I'm Chavonne

                     WES
Hi Chavonne I'm Wes

                   CHAVONNE
What song are you hearing today?

                              WES
Oh---uhm it's called Zombie!

                           CHAVONNE
Ew! They're so gross!

                              WES
It's a cool song though by Fela Kuti

It's about how people just do what they are told without
thinking about it.

                           CHAVONNE
Really?

                              WES
Yup. And it's got the coolest beat. Here

                    Wes puts an earbud in her ear and we see
                    Chavonne light up

                           CHAVONNE
Cool.

                              WES
Right!?

                           CHAVONNE
I love music but I like science more

                              WES
Science is cool

                           CHAVONNE
I think its messed up they call you that name

14

                              WES

It doesn't bother me

                           CHAVONNE

Name calling isn't nice

                              WES

I don't pay attention

                           CHAVONNE

How can you not pay attention

                        Wes shrugs

                              WES

I'm too busy listening to the music
Here's another song I like…

                           CHAVONNE

And ever since I known him that's been his attitude. It's
what I like the most about him

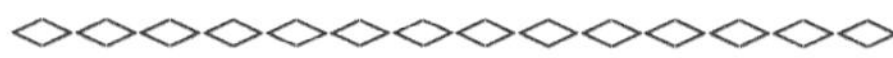

                              WES

Chavonne, come on, are you gonna play? They're gonna be
picking teams

                           CHAVONNE

I don't know --doesn't it bother you?

                              WES

What?

CHAVONNE

Getting picked last

WES

There are worse things

CHAVONNE

Than being picked last?

WES

Allergic to grass
An itchy halloween mask
A long list of chores and menial tasks
time machine leaving you stuck in past
All worse than being picked last

TEAM CAPTAINS

There's nothing worse
Nothing worse
No there's nothing worse

WES

Being hit in your lip with a ball of brass
Locked in an elevator with someone crass
There are plenty things worse than being picked last

TEAM CAPTAINS

No there's nothing worse
No there's nothing worse

WES

A chocolate fast?

TEAM CAPTAINS

No nothing worse

WES

I don't think its that big a deal

CHAVONNE

But it is a big deal because—remember we talked about the cornbread? And the butterflies

.

Last night, Wes doesn't know this, but last night. I had a vision, not a dream.

FREUD

Yo I got em'
What it do, ya man Freud back with another one. This gon be a lot for ya head talk but aye---each one teach one, m-i-riiiiiight? So lets go

While highly contested and debated Dreams and Visions have distinct differences. Dreams are involuntary. As you sleep the brain begins to offload the day's experiences. Whatever you seem to recall you call a dream. A vision occurs while waking, and while in some ways also involuntary, it is tied to a logic and can often be the catalyst for action steps.

CHAVONNE

Right. Get all that?

My vision

So
So
So

The first flap of the butterfly wing

CHAVONNE (cont)
Wes gets picked before the new kid
And this kid is brand brand new
No idea what his game's like
No idea what he can do

So Wes'll think

WES
Dang ! Darn! Why do I even try
So later for this blacktop, bye

CHAVONNE
So he tries to go back inside
And the teachers say

MRS. YANCY
Wes you can't come back inside
Stay out, you must play

WES
Nah it's not my scene
Enough Captains and teams!
I got dreams, skills
and schemes, schemes, schemes

MRS. YANCY
I'm gonna call your parents
We have concern for you
With that attitude
No tellin' what you might do

CHAVONNE
They've worried Wes's folks
Who have no patience
They pull him out of school
And then relocate him

WES

But the new place is even worse
They pick me last there too
I run away like you expect
High tail off into the blue

CHAVONNE

And off in the blue
Feeling lost and beat
All alone along the road
Until he begins to meet

STRANGER 1

Criss crossin

STRANGER 2

Backpackin

STRANGER 1

Safe crackin'

STRANGER 2

Shady-shannon blokes

STRANGER 1

The Laid Off

STRANGER 2

Played Off

STRANGER 1

Gruff

STRANGER 2

Rough Tumblin folks

STRANGER 1

Bumblin'

STRANGER 2

Bar room Rumblin'

CHAVONNE

Nature's cruel jokes!

WES

But there is a common core
Don't take much to grasp

STRANGERS 1, 2 & WES

We were on the playground
We all got picked last!

CHAVONNE

So he feels a kinship
with this scrappy crew
turns fully to the bad life
He's been adopted to

WES

My solutions
Open doors
That're locked
Holding treasure

My solutions
May hurt others
But bring me so much pleasure

Now I decide
What will or wont happen
Life is just a game
Now I'M the Team Captain

TEAM CAPTAIN CLAIRE
Don't hurt us Wes!

TEAM CAPTAIN BILAL
Come on Wes be fair!

WES
I pick you BOTH to be first
To a life of despair

CHAVONNE
No Wes No!

WES
Now that I think about it, I pick YOU first Chavonne
You were my friend
You let them pick me last
Day after day

CHAVONNE
Wes, no Wes, come on I am your friend!

WES
Friends!?
Who needs them!

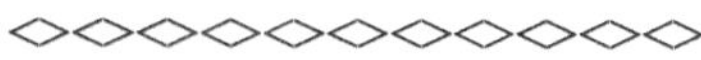

FREUD
I don't know Chavonne. Sounds more like a nightmare than a vision.

CHAVONNE
Get outta here Freud!

Exit Freud grumbling under his breath

CHAVONNE

Ugh--I can't seem to connect the right dots, to make this plan
work--it was all so clear to me before but now I just feel
stuck!

GRACE HOPPER

That means it's working!

CHAVONNE

Huh---Oh my….are you?

GRACE HOPPER

Hey there Chavonne

NEW KID

Whoa Admiral Grace Hopper goes to school here?

GRACE HOPPER

Oh no, no--I'm just here to help Chavonne

CHAVONNE

(to New Kid)
I think it's really cool you know who this is but I'm kind of
in the middle of something right now

NEW KID

Oh, right, sure. Catch ya later

CHAVONNE

(To Grace)
Sorry. New Kid---you know

GRACE HOPPER

Been there!
Sounds like you got a bug in your processor

CHAVONNE

Of course! You were the first computerist to find a bug ever,
right?

GRACE HOPPER

Not exactly, folks like Edison had used that word *bug* long
time ago. But yea, my team we found a moth between the
relay contacts of the Harvard Mark II
 You know computers were massive back in those days,
surprised we didn't get squirrels back there too!

Chavonne gives a chortle

GRACE HOPPER

But I'm here to tell you that the bugs are part of it. That
moth could feel the heat coming out those rooms and
naturally gravitated to it!

CHAVONNE

I'm not following

GRACE HOPPER

If you're not making mistakes, you're not taking risks, and
that means you're not going anywhere. You're making
change, no, you writing a whole new code

CHAVONNE

When you were creating the first compiler I bet people
thought you were wasting your time

GRACE

Of course. As a woman in the Navy, people wanted me to
just handle clerical work and all I wanted to do was build
machines that could think.

CHAVONNE
What did you do when you got stuck?

GRACE

You get yourself unstuck! You take a risk. Just keep going.
That's the key. You know what we did with that moth we
found. We taped it to our report, in tribute. That lil guy gave
his life for progress--we went from computers taking up
room after room, to computers thousands of times more
powerful on your wristwatch!

CHAVONNE

Did you ever think it was possible

GRACE

Of course I did. Because anything is possible.

> *Chavonne stands and salutes the Admiral who
> salutes back.*

CHAVONNE

You got this

> *Exit Grace*

> *We hear a fly buzzing. Chavonne follows it with
> her eyes. Picks up something to swat it, and the
> bug buzzes itself away.*

CHAVONNE

That's right bug. Not today.

..

..

◇◇◇◇◇◇◇◇◇◇◇◇

CHAVONNE

Claire

                    TEAM CAPTAIN CLAIRE
Chavonne
 I look forward to seeing you on the blacktop later

                        CHAVONNE
Yeeeeeaaaaa about that…

                    TEAM CAPTAIN CLAIRE
What? You're not going to recess now?

                        CHAVONNE
Of course. Gotta get that fresh air and exercise
No it's just that I don't think I wanna play the game

                    TEAM CAPTAIN CLAIRE
Well why not? Games are fun.

                        CHAVONNE
Sure sure, it's just that, well, nevermind

                    TEAM CAPTAIN CLAIRE
What?

                        CHAVONNE
I'm no snitch and you know what they say

                    TEAM CAPTAIN CLAIRE
That snitches get stitches?

                        CHAVONNE
That's what they say

                    TEAM CAPTAIN CLAIRE
We've known each other since 3rd grade

                        CHAVONNE
Yes

TEAM CAPTAIN CLAIRE
I always felt we had a good relationship

CHAVONNE
I mean…

TEAM CAPTAIN CLAIRE
Oh you're not still hanging on to that ---misunderstanding
are you?

CHAVONNE
It was pretty awful.

TEAM CAPTAIN CLAIRE
But I said I was sorry

CHAVONNE
You didn't

TEAM CAPTAIN CLAIRE
I didn't?

CHAVONNE
And you still haven't

TEAM CAPTAIN CLAIRE
My memory of things is different

CHAVONNE
Okay

Chavonne feigns an exit

TEAM CAPTAIN CLAIRE
Wait wait wait

CHAVONNE

What?

TEAM CAPTAIN CLAIRE

Are you going to tell me?

CHAVONNE

I don't know...am I?

TEAM CAPTAIN CLAIRE

(Sigh)

CHAVONNE

Come on. You'll feel better.

TEAM CAPTAIN CLAIRE

Fine.
(breath)
I'm sorry Chavonne

CHAVONNE

For what?

TEAM CAPTAIN CLAIRE

For what I said about you in 3rd grade

CHAVONNE

Thank you Claire. I appreciate that apology...sounded *real* sincere too

TEAM CAPTAIN CLAIRE

Okay tell me tell me

CHAVONNE

Alright but I'm not a rumor starter

TEAM CAPTAIN CLAIRE
Tell me TELL me TELL ME!!

CHAVONNE
You ever heard of sports betting

TEAM CAPTAIN CLAIRE
Sports betting?

CHAVONNE
Yes. Like gambling.

TEAM CAPTAIN CLAIRE
I guess

CHAVONNE
Well, I can't say who, but I heard certain ---grown ups who are supposed to be instilling strong values in us have been betting on the outcomes of our games

TEAM CAPTAIN CLAIRE
Betting?

CHAVONNE
So for example

◇◇◇◇◇◇◇◇◇◇◇

TWFTPOTPWRA[1]
Today it's Kickball okay
And I'm gonna clean up! Cha-to-the-CHING!
Wanna know how I know? Wannaknow?
Go head ask me, ask me….okay I'll tell you

Tim Jenkins is a great kicker
A great kicker indeed, been clockin that kid since 2nd grade

---

[1] Teacher Who For The Purposes Of This Play Will Remain Anonymous

Kid could kick a hole through the atmosphere, kick a ball to
the moon

I'm telling you---I guarantee Team Captain Claire picks him
first!

How do I know? How do I know?
 O-M-to the G, that girl is so predictable
Not that I'm complaining I been making a pretty penny
A pretty penny INDEED off of her choices

TEAM CAPTAIN CLAIRE
A pretty penny indeed!?

CHAVONNE
Yea

TEAM CAPTAIN CLAIRE
Gambling on school grounds is illegal and inappropriate
And I will not be a part of that

CHAVONNE
Well there's only one way to stop it

TEAM CAPTAIN CLAIRE
Right!
.
What is it?

CHAVONNE
He says you're predictable so you gotta be unpredictable

TEAM CAPTAIN CLAIRE
Right

CHAVONNE
He knows who you always pick

TEAM CAPTAIN CLAIRE
I don't always pick the same…

CHAVONNE
Stacy, please read it back...

Stacy, the play stenographer checks the text

STACY
(reading)

TEAM CAPTAIN BILAL
I'll take Isis

TEAM CAPTAIN CLAIRE
I'll take Tim

TEAM CAPTAIN BILAL
I'll take Hector

TEAM CAPTAIN CLAIRE
Julia

TEAM CAPTAIN BILAL
Quincy

TEAM CAPTAIN CLAIRE
Okay I get it

CHAVONNE
Look it's probably not that serious--people talk you know

TEAM CAPTAIN CLAIRE

Are you kidding?

CHAVONNE

We're just kids playin' games at recess

TEAM CAPTAIN CLAIRE

Chavonne…. I'm a team captain

That's everything

They look to me to choose
Whether we win whether we lose
I need to have picked the best I could
They look to me to choose

I'd be a silly fool
If I just picked my amigos
I need someone who can shoot a three
And someone who makes free throws

Someone who can dodge the ball
Someone who can throw
Not just my buds and chums
Not just the folks I know

CHAVONNE

You always pick Wes last
And that's what's to be expected
Now that you know the devious scheme
Do your best to reject it

TEAM CAPTAIN CLAIRE

What are you saying Chavonne?

CHAVONNE

It's really an easy ask
Instead of your usual choice
Of Wes
What if you pick me last!

TEAM CAPTAIN CLAIRE

But Bilal always picks you second to last

CHAVONNE

Right! So maybe pick Wes sooner!

TEAM CAPTAIN CLAIRE

Pick Wes earlier? People'll think I went Looner!

CHAVONNE

the goals to be unpredictable
and you never know
you pick Wes maybe third to last
Bilal won't know which way to go---
he'll be flustered thinking why did Claire do as she did
And maybe he doesn't select me and picks the new kid

TEAM CAPTAIN CLAIRE

What New Kid?

NEW KID

Hey--

TEAM CAPTAIN CLAIRE

How long have you been standing there?

NEW KID

My family and I just got here. What a cool town this is…

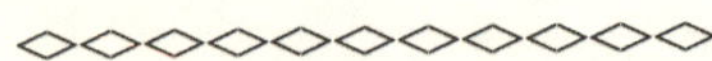

TEAM CAPTAIN BILAL
The New Kid? What about him.

CHAVONNE
Just thought you should know—New Kid has got-some-
game!

TEAM CAPTAIN BILAL
Oh yeah? What games?

CHAVONNE
Everything!

TEAM CAPTAIN BILAL
Everything like what?

CHAVONNE
You know--all the stuff we play

TEAM CAPTAIN BILAL
Oh really?

CHAVONNE
Yes!

TEAM CAPTAIN BILAL
Because I asked the new kid "Sup, what do you like to play"
"You any good?"

NEW KID
I like to get out there and get fresh air. Have a good time

TEAM CAPTAIN BILAL
Made me wanna throw up!

CHAVONNE
Look New Kid comes from a place where boasting and
bragging is very unpopular

TEAM CAPTAIN BILAL
Telling folks how formidable you are at sports is not
bragging and boasting
The facts are the facts

CHAVONNE
And fact is...the new kid is --what do they call it...A
PROBLEM

TEAM CAPTAIN BILAL
Hmmm…

CHAVONNE
Well you know what? Maybe don't take a chance
Claire will pick for her team and if New Kid is actually not
that good—*boom!*
Works out for you BUT if New Kid turns out to be as good
as I know ….

TEAM CAPTAIN BILAL
Yea.

CHAVONNE
Think it over

◇◇◇◇◇◇
CHAVONNE
My plan was gonna work
…

                              WES
I see what you're doing.

                           CHAVONNE
What am I doing?

                              WES
Manipulating

                           CHAVONNE
I don't know what you're talking about.

                              WES
It's really not a big deal.

                           CHAVONNE
It is

                              WES
I'm fine to be picked last

                           CHAVONNE
No you're not

                              WES
No. You're not fine with me being picked last.

                           CHAVONNE
Fine! I'm not.

                              WES
Let it go Chavonne. You're starting to embarrass me.
It's like you're trying to be my agent or something

                           CHAVONNE
I'm being your friend.

WES

I didn't ask for this. And I don't want it.
I'm not a charity case

CHAVONNE

Trust me okay. It's gonna be great. Bilal will take Isis. Claire
will take Tim. Bilal will take Hector. Claire will take Julia.
Bilal will take Quincy. Then Claire will take YOU then Bilal
will take the New Kid and Claire will pick me last! And
you'll see Wes. You'll feel the difference.

WES

Chavonne just stop

CHAVONNE

It's already planned. It's in motion. Trust me.

WES

Well then I won't play

CHAVONNE

Of course you will. You have to. Look I'm sick of people
treating you like a loser

WES

I don't care. I'm not.

CHAVONNE

Look I read this article one time from this famous important
woman, an ambassador or something. She said she never
forgot how she was always the last to be chosen for a team.
She said it made her embarrassed and feel pathetic.

WES

But she became an important woman, an ambassador

CHAVONNE

Well yeah but…

WES

Being picked first or last---it's not gonna matter. So stop
meddling.

CHAVONNE

But it DOES

WES

Chavonne this is about you not me. I just like to play

CHAVONNE

It's not meddling

Wes just shakes his head and walks off

CHAVONNE

It's not meddling Wes! You'll see. You'll feel the difference!

EDWARD LORENZ

You're making a rookie mistake

CHAVONNE

Oh you again

EDWARD LORENZ

The butterfly effect is always in effect. You can't undo things
or try and steer. Even inaction is an action

MRS. YANCY

That's a very evocative point

CHAVONNE

I got it

FREUD
In many ways this reminds me of the ongoing debate
between the free will versus determinism the extent to which
our behavior is the result of forces over which we have no
control or whether people are able to decide for themselves
whether to act or behave in a certain way

EDWARD LORENZ
I don't think it's really about that---

MRS. YANCY
It's a stretch but I think perhaps what Freud is getting at is---

CHAVONNE
Hey hey hey---all of you---I need to think---please ---buzz
off

They all start talking at once

CHAVONNE
GOOOOOOOOOOOOOOOOO!!!

They quietly exit

CHAVONNE
He'll see.

The bell rings
It's recess---
We see the Team Captains take their positions

CHAVONNE
Wes?!
Wes?!

Hey can we -

TEAM CAPTAIN CLAIRE

Wanna go first?

CHAVONNE

Wait—Wes isn't here—I know he wants to play

TEAM CAPTAIN BILAL

We only get 22 minutes Chavonne

NEW KID

Excuse me. Hi.

TEAM CAPTAIN CLAIRE

You're the new kid right?

NEW KID

Yes! So happy to be here. So look, I'm just curious, what is your selection
process for Team Captains? Do you rotate? Is by vote? Is it teacher assigned

TEAM CAPTAIN BILAL

What?

NEW KID

Well I assume it's not just you two and team captains every time that would be…(chuckle)

TEAM CAPTAIN CLAIRE

Why wouldn't it be

NEW KID

Well….because…I'm sorry I don't want to offend but where I come from
Our team captains change

CHAVONNE
That's not a bad idea if you ask me

TEAM CAPTAIN BILAL
Nobody asked you

WES
I agree.

CHAVONNE
Hey Wes I thought you weren't coming?

WES
Mrs. Yancy told me I had to stay out here
I was gonna count the acorns but then I heard New Kid

NEW KID
My name is…

WES
His idea is a good one. You need to listen to this new kid

TEAM CAPTAIN CLAIRE
Well of course you would. You always get picked last!

NEW KID
Is that true?

WES
Yeah but it's no big deal

NEW KID
It is to me.

New Kid begins to exit

TEAM CAPTAIN BILAL

You gonna go tattle-tell on us?

NEW KID

No of course not. Where I come from we have a saying…

CHAVONNE

Snitches get stitches?

NEW KID

Indeed they do. But more than that, where I come from we believe in equity

TEAM CAPTAIN BILAL

Ewwwwww

CHAVONNE

Do you even know what that word means?

TEAM CAPTAIN BILAL

No. Shut up.

NEW KID

Just means he goes first
And she goes next
Then I go, then he go
We all get to flex
A portion for you
Her and me
That be the recipe for equity

TEAM CAPTAIN BILAL

Sounds more like socialism

WES

Socialism is a system
Equity is an ism
An idea where all colors shine

NEW KID

Prism!

WES

You're pretty cool New Kid

Hey lets' start our own game

NEW KID

Splendid!

TEAM CAPTAIN CLAIRE

What?

NEW KID

Wes you should be Captain

WES

I don't have to be

TEAM CAPTAIN BILAL

No way!

CHAVONNE

Yes way! Wes what you think?

WES

Sure…..do we know what game we're playing yet?

NEW KID

I can teach you all this great game we played in my old
town. It's pretty wild

42

CHAVONNE

Sounds perfect

TEAM CAPTAIN BILAL

You're gonna just adopt some strange foreign game

WES

Chavonne---be the other Captain

NEW KID

That sounds great! You seem like a natural leader

CHAVONNE

Aw shucks y'all---I just---you know like to get my fresh air

TEAM CAPTAIN CLAIRE

What is happening!?

NEW KID

Anybody else wanna be a part of our game?

WES

Who wants to play?

TEAM CAPTAIN BILAL

Stop

TEAM CAPTAIN CLAIRE

We're the team captains

WES

Of that game. We're playing our game over here.

NEW KID

Democracy. Equity. I feel so at home.

CHAVONNE

Eating cornbread in bed causes car accidents
A butterfly flapping its wings could cause an earthquake in Japan
Getting picked last can cause some problems for people

But eating cornbread in bed can also help you sleep
And teach you a lot about ants
A butterfly flapping its wings can also make the flowers grow
Getting picked last in one game, means you can become team captain of another

EDWARD LORENZ

Yo this kid really gets it!

FREUD

You're telling me.

NEW KID

(addressing the audience)
Hey do you guys wanna play?

CHAVONNE

You can see them too?

WES

Sure. We all love science!

Okay, I'll take Edward Lorenz!

CHAVONNE

I'll take Freud

They continue to pick teams and begin a game derived by the ensemble, it can be entirely made up, perhaps there's some role the audience can play? Maybe a verbal response to a call of some kind or a clap or stomp. It needn't be too complicated.

The game play will serve as the closing image/ moment of this show.